SLAYING YOUR
WEEKEND WARRIOR

AN ALTERNATIVE APPROACH TO ABSTINENCE

*"No eternal reward will forgive us
now for wasting the dawn."*

–Jim Morrison

SLAYING YOUR
WEEKEND WARRIOR

AN ALTERNATIVE APPROACH TO ABSTINENCE

CREATED BY
FRANK HALL

Love. Peace. Clarity. Wisdom. Strength.

Dedications

For my family. Mom, Dad, Kerrie, and James.

For my heroes. Sergio, Angie, and Jimmy.

For my dearest Maria.

And for my closest of friends.

I am eternally grateful for all of your unconditional love and kindness. I love you all.

Special thanks and my deepest gratitude to Dawn Bossman who undertook the job of editing this book with tender care and an open mind. Namaste. Om.

Special thanks and my sincerest appreciation for Courtney Miller who created the artwork for this book. You are extremely creative and talented.

Table Of Contents

• i •

Introduction

1

• I •

Ground Zero

7

• II •

Getting to Know Your Weekend Warrior

17

• III •

Habits, Hobbies, and Routines

23

• IV •

Reaping The Benefits

31

• V •

Maintaining Motivation

39

• VI •

Becoming Your Own Hero

47

Introduction

IT IS NO SECRET THAT ALCOHOL consumption is a cornerstone to many of the leisure activities that we partake in as a society. There will never be a shortage of light beers at the ball games and there will always be plenty of "Jame-o" shots and Red Bull Vodkas to keep us on the dance floor of McKenzie McFlannery's until the wee hours of morning. However, we have become so accustomed to the "normality" of alcohol consumption that in many cases we lose sight of the dangers and consequences from the poor choices that we make on our weekend escapades. Many of us know these consequences all too well and so here we are. Searching for a way to better ourselves and make a change. That change my dear friends is abstinence. No more alcohol. Say it with me. No more alcohol.

When I made my decision to end my eleven-and-a-half-year hall of fame career as a drinker, I wasn't sure where to begin. Initially, I thought about attending AA meetings or seeking therapy for my feelings of depression. But after careful consideration and some admitted stubbornness, I decided that I would try my own approach before doing anything else. Fortunately, my do-it-yourself (DIY) method of quitting drinking was a lot easier than I had anticipated. In fact, it was almost too easy.

With that being said, I didn't just wake up hung over one morning and say, "That's it, I am never drinking again," and then ride off into the sunset. I had to discover what my triggers were. I had to unlearn the habits that kept me going back for more drinks. I had to do the homework on myself. I decided to look inward for the answers that I desperately sought. This left me playing the role of the teacher and the student at the same time. It was an extremely rewarding experience and one of the best decisions that I have ever made. While there is an abundant amount of information pertaining to alcohol abuse online and in the local libraries, I felt that a lot of the material that I was reading did not directly correlate to my circumstances. This was discouraging at first, but it would ultimately lead to some of my finest self-reflections and in short, this crash course on abstinence that I have prepared for you.

As I began to understand my weekly routines, I came to recognize that my entire problem lied in the weekends. I rarely drank on weeknights, and if I did, it would usually be a couple of beers or a few glasses of wine. Nothing out of the "ordinary." However, my weekdays of consistency were completely thrown into disarray as soon as the workweek would end on Friday afternoons. On my way home from work, I would grab the first tall boy I could get my hands on, and from there on I'd pretty much drink the weekends straight through. I'm talking about full-blown weekend benders.

Whether it was bars, parties, shows, brunches, sporting events, or days at the beach, there was a high probability that you would find me somewhere out there as drunk as a lord. Sure it may sound nice on paper, and yes there were plenty of fun times in the mix, but at the end of the day I was utterly miserable. I was unfulfilled and I was leading a life that was becoming progressively unbearable. The choice became obvious. I had to find consistency in my routines. I had to stay vigilant. I had to be true to my core beliefs and morals. I had to unify my feelings and principles with my actions at all times. I had to face my demons and I had to slay my Weekend Warrior.

One of the conclusions I made was that a lot of my personal habits and a good chunk of our society's habits relating to alcohol consumption do not pair with those of the "conventional alcoholic" and therefore should be treated as such. For that reason alone, this will be the last time that you see the word alcoholic in this book. I firmly believe that many of the traditional approaches to maintaining abstinence are very rigid and outdated, so I organized this concise "cookbook" for achieving an alcohol free life in our modern society. I have provided you with the ingredients and the recipe for success, but the outcome depends on you and you alone. If you want to be successful on your road to abstinence, you have to genuinely want it for yourself.

This book will be your guide, not your bible. This book will be your best tool and at times your favorite weapon to utilize should you ever feel the urge or desire to drink alcohol. This is an alternative do-it-yourself approach that focuses on moving forward and rolling with positive momentum rather than dwelling in the past.

We are not just quitting drinking here. We will be creating healthy and productive daily routines, as well as rediscovering our true passions with thorough and extensive self-reflection. Although this is an important transitional process in our lives that we must handle with care, we must also remember to have fun with it. Abandoning the booze does not need to be all doom and gloom. This is an exciting adventure, so make it fun. I mean after all, it's not everyday that we get to have a spiritual awakening of the soul.

In the upcoming chapters you will learn who your Weekend Warrior is. You will learn how to fight against the cycle that has been slowly sucking the life out of you and preventing you from reaching your full potential. We will discuss quitting drinking in its early stages as well as how to maintain motivation and remain abstinent long term. I have designed a four-month timeline with course questions and challenges at the end of each chapter for you to carefully complete and answer honestly. These are the questions and challenges that I found exceptionally valuable in my personal journey and wish to share with you. Some of these methods are a bit unorthodox so do not feel pressured into completing anything that you feel uncomfortable with. Although it is advised, you do not have to adhere to the four-month reading timeline. We all move at our own pace. This is your story. You do the work. You make the rules. Just know that if you really want alcohol out of your life, you will be able to overcome this bump in the road and every aspect of your life will begin to change in ways that you would have never imagined. All aboard the wagon. Fly straight and have a great.

Take Note: If your body is heavily dependent on alcohol, quitting drinking cold turkey can be dangerous. Visit your doctor or seek rehabilitation if you are experiencing serious withdrawals.

I

Ground Zero

"Mistakes are the portals of discovery."

-James Joyce

FOR JUST ONE MOMENT, I WANT you to put away all of your feelings of anxiety, guilt, regret, and sorrow. However you may be feeling right now, I want you to know that this is as bad as it gets should you decide to remain abstinent. But right now you are hung over and you look like hell. So go take a cold shower, grab a vanilla iced coffee and get back over here.

Alright, let's get into it. We are at ground zero. Up to this point you have spent a lot of your free time drinking and partaking in mindless activities. I will make the assumption that things are not going quite as well for you as you had planned, and you are now aware that your drinking habits are the primary cause for your suffering. Boom! You did it! You just quit drinking, more or less.

Although I am not a big advocate for AA, I will say that they hit the nail right on the head when it comes to acceptance. Taking ownership of your actions and being aware of your strengths and weaknesses is a wonderful character trait to have, not only in remaining abstinent but also in life in general. There is a significant power in self-awareness, and being honest with yourself will give you a stupendous advantage in defeating your Weekend Warrior. On the other hand, if you do not take care of the issues at foot, things will tend to get worse. It's just like using a broken toilet over and over again. The shit starts to pile up. That's some pleasant imagery, wouldn't you say? Now then; when you can look at yourself from an impartial standpoint and make honest self-reflections, you become the true master of your mind. You become fully in control of your thoughts and actions. And when temptations come your way, you will triumph because you will be prepared for them. Personal awareness is the key that will open up the door to your new and improved lifestyle.

Now that I gave AA their time of day, I feel completely comfortable contrasting their approach with the one that you are about to read. But before I continue, I must say that what they have done and continue to do for people throughout the years is nothing short of astonishing. Their approach works for thousands upon thousands of individuals and that is truly wonderful. If it works for you, than by all means stick to it. However, it would appear that you are searching for something different. You might be looking for an approach that is more "up your alley." Trust me, I get it. When I first started down my road to abstinence, I had been searching for that something as well, but I couldn't find it. So I created it. And now it is here for you to peruse through and expand upon.

Slaying Your Weekend Warrior and AA differ in many ways but the main difference begins with one pivotal gripe that I have against them. AA says that you have to surrender to a higher power and admit defeat to your alcoholism, whereas I believe you have all of the skills that you need right inside of you to successfully remain abstinent. One of AA's twelve steps states that we must "admit we were powerless over alcohol—that our lives have become unmanageable." Sorry for my vulgarity, but personally I think that statement is a load of shit. Most of us who deal with alcohol related issues already tend to have a problem with self-confidence, so admitting that we are powerless over alcohol could potentially do more harm to us than good. As long as the alcohol remains on the shelf and in the bottle, we are one hundred percent in power over it. It really is that simple. Plus, if we are going to take the blame for the mistakes that we have made in our past, then you better damn well believe that we will be taking the credit for the positive life that we create for ourselves in our present and future. You are always in control of your thoughts and actions. Once again, you are the master of your mind. Do not ever forget that.

I explained in the introduction that this is a do-it-yourself (DIY) approach. And while I will give my personal opinions from time to time, none of what I say is "The word of God" truth. There may be instances in which something that has worked for me will not resonate with you and that is totally fine. I compel you to challenge and question everything that you hear, see, and read. This will keep you engaged and growing on your journey. If the only flavor of ice cream was pistachio, then I wouldn't like ice cream. But thanks to vanilla, chocolate, cookies and cream, and toasted almond, I can happily say that I am a fan of ice cream. The point that I am trying to make here is that there are multiple ways to achieve your objective. Some methods will work better for you than others. It's just a different flavor of ice cream. There is no perfect equation, but you have to take the approach that you believe will work best for you. We all have different philosophies, mentalities, beliefs, and ways in which we motivate ourselves, but in the end we share the same goal: an alcohol free life.

Depending on how long you have been drinking, even the very thought of an alcohol free life could sound intimidating at first. It is natural to be afraid of change, but you cannot continue to limit yourself with a substance that will never bring any true value or light into your life. The path to abstinence and inner peace will begin once you take that first step out of your comfort zone and learn to embrace life in a new, healthy, positive, and productive manner.

Out of the gate, you might notice that you will be asking yourself many internal questions such as, "What will my friends think?" To be honest, you will most likely get mixed feedback depending upon your group of friends. Your buddies who know you best will usually be completely supportive of your decision. There is a good chance that they know how you have been feeling lately, and they will have your best interests at heart—maybe, maybe not. Some people may laugh at you and say some sarcastic crap like, "Oh yeah, we'll see how long this lasts." Please do yourself a favor early on; do not listen to any negativity whatsoever. Opinions are like assholes bud, everybody's got one. When push comes to shove, it really doesn't matter what anyone thinks. This is your time to shine. You know what your true intentions are, and you have to keep your focus on your purpose: an alcohol free life.

"What will I do on the weekends now that I don't drink?" Depending on your willpower, and I will repeat, depending on your willpower, I would recommend you *initially* try doing the same activities but without the drinking. Go to the bars and remain alcohol free. This may not seem like the best idea, but when you are sober at a bar or a party you may just begin to see all of the things that you hated about yourself in some of the other people that are out and about. This is not to say you should go out and judge these people and become the condescending sober douche (CSD). Personally, I have much more respect for the drunkards at the bar than the CSDs. But yeah, I'm just saying to be observant. Notice the excessiveness and the ugliness of the people who have had too much to drink and are no longer in control of themselves. Notice the need for instant gratification, the selfish desires, and the irrational behaviors that are going on around you. You will begin to see that the once "normal" lifestyle that you had become so accustomed to is in fact very abnormal and unsettling. You may even feel like Ebenezer Scrooge after meeting the ghost of Christmas past in the Charles Dickens classic "A Christmas Carol." Sometimes it is necessary to face the ugly truth in order to learn a beautiful and humbling lesson. But as I said, you have to have the willpower to remain alcohol free should you decide to hang out in such a setting. Do you remember the repentant words of Mr. Scrooge's deceased business partner, Jacob Marley, when he speaks of the metaphorical chains that he is forced to carry in his afterlife? "I wear the chain I forged in life. I made it link by link, and yard by yard. I girded it on of my own free will, and of my own free will I wore it." When you become aware of your poor habits and see with a clear mind the limitations that you have bestowed upon yourself, you can finally break free from the heavy chain that you have been burdening yourself with for all this time. Once that chain is gone, you can then begin to fully explore your true passions. With that, you will be able to live a more fulfilling lifestyle, and just like Ebenezer Scrooge you will have successfully granted yourself a second chance at life.

"Will I still feel miserable even after I stop drinking?" Once your hangover subsides, you will notice yourself feeling a little bit better each day. Alcohol dulls all of your senses and toys with your emotions. After only a few days you will start to reap the rewards in major ways. What I would strongly recommend is to not let the benefits overwhelm you. I know that this may sound silly to you, but what I mean by this is to try not to get ahead of yourself. After a few weeks you will start to feel like you can accomplish anything you set out to do, and you can. However, do not make the mistake of trying to do everything at once. Spend your early stages of abstinence focusing on your affirmations of alcohol free living. Once you feel comfortable with that, you can take another step, and then another. Do not try to take on multiple tasks at once.

There is a philosophical paradox known as "Burden's Ass" which tells the moral story of a donkey who is equally hungry and thirsty. He is placed between a stack of hay and a pail of water. Because he cannot make up his mind as to where he will go first, he fails to act entirely and eventually dies of starvation and thirst. Make no mistake about it, you can accomplish any and all of your goals, but you cannot accomplish them all at once. Prioritize your goals and take it slow. Have patience, young padawan. You will get there.

Right now the wounds are fresh. It hurts. Let it hurt. Excessive alcohol consumption cripples and destroys relationships, sabotages careers and potential opportunities. It deteriorates your health, leads to legal and financial burdens, and opens up the door to a myriad of other problems. For what exactly? Absolutely nothing. Alcohol will never benefit you in any way. It is an unnecessary part of life and it will hold you back from reaching your full potential so long as you continue to partake. If you choose to remain alcohol free however, you will start to shine brighter than the North fn star.

I challenge you now to invite back those emotions of sadness, guilt and regret. Feel how painful it is and remember this feeling. Pause for a moment to reflect. Now take comfort in knowing that you will never feel this amount of disparity again, but please never forget how it feels. For maintaining long-term sobriety it is crucial to remind ourselves of how we felt when we decided to break our habitual drinking habits. Reliving and revisiting the emotions that we felt in our early stages of abstinence will help keep us motivated down the road. This will prove to be an invaluable tool in slaying your Weekend Warrior. But before we get to know just who that bastard truly is, take some time to get yourself a notebook and a pen. It is now time to answer and perform the Chapter I questions and reflections. Really take your time with this and be completely honest and thorough with yourself. This is your internal home-work. After two weeks of sobriety and self-reflective journaling, begin Chapter II. Fly straight and have a great.

Ground Zero: Questions and Reflections

1. How do I feel right now?

2. What problems have I encountered in my life because of my habitual drinking routines?

3. When did I start drinking and why?

4. Why do I want to stop drinking?

5. Where do I see myself in four months if I continue to drink alcohol?

6. Where do I see myself in four months if I extinguish alcohol from my life?

- Eliminate alcohol
- Drink water. Stay hydrated.

Challenges:

Go out with your friends and remain alcohol free. Document your feelings and observations.

Establish a healthy and productive daily routine. Document results daily.

II

Getting to Know Your Weekend Warrior

TWO WEEKS OF ABSTINENCE

"Being able to quit things that don't work is integral to being a winner."

-Timothy Ferriss

WHEN FIGHTING IN A WAR, IT is imperative that you under-stand the enemy. The more you know about your adversary, the greater your chances will be in defeating him/her. In this case you are fighting an internal war and you are your own enemy. You are getting in your own way and this is preventing you from living a life of consistent happiness and prosperity. It is vital that you find out what triggers you. What is it exactly that makes you crave alco-hol? Do you drink out of boredom? Do you drink to avoid facing reality? Do you drink because you are just used to the same old weekend routines? This answer will vary from person to person but whatever the reasons are, you must figure them out. This will prepare you for situations where you may be caught off guard by an opportunity to drink. By understanding your triggers, you give yourself the upper hand in breaking poor drinking habits.

As I mentioned earlier, my initial trigger was grabbing a tall boy on the way home from work on Friday afternoons. The first few days of abstinence for me proved difficult when I walked by all of the beer stands in Penn Station and resisted the chance to catch that quick buzz on my train ride home. But what I had begun to realize after a few days was quite funny actually. I wasn't really craving the alcohol at all. I had just been thirsty from working so hard during the day, and I needed something to quench my thirst. Once I made that Sherlock Holmes-esque discovery, I replaced my tall beer with a large fruit smoothie or freshly squeezed lemonade and my thirst was quenched all the same. Just like that, one of my Weekend Warriors habits was broken. By taking a few moments to be conscious of my thought process, I was able to identify a problem and solve it. Simple as that. You will make many self-discoveries like this as you continue down your own path of sobriety. So embrace these positive changes, learn as much as you can about your triggers, and have fun with it. This is your chance to rediscover your true passions and regain a newfound appreciation for life.

Unfortunately, your Weekend Warrior has other plans and will not go down without a fight. You have accumulated many unacceptable drinking habits that you will need to break, and triggers that you will have to uncover. Your Weekend Warrior is going to look for any reason to persuade you to have a drink. "You can have one or two." No you can't. "A glass of wine with dinner is fine. And they say it's healthy for you." No it isn't. "You haven't drank in so long. Just have a few. See? You proved you could stop whenever you want." Wrong. We are not training our minds for moderation. We are training for abstinence, so it is important to be prepared at all times. You cannot let your guard down for a second. Alcohol is everywhere. And unless you plan on becoming a recluse, you are going to be around it on many occasions. So you'd better get used to it. You will face temptations from your Weekend Warrior as well as your family, friends, and co-workers. Holidays and birthdays will be tough. Major events such as weddings will test you. Especially those godforsaken open bars. How will you handle these moments of temptation?

Preparation is the answer to this question. Preparation will defeat temptation. If you know you will be attending an event where alcohol will be readily available, take the necessary steps to prepare yourself. Know roughly when you are going to arrive and know when you are going to leave. Know what you are going to do while you are at the event. Think about what you are going to eat and drink. The more you prepare yourself for facing temptations, the easier it will be to remain vigilant once those situations present themselves.

Another tactic your Weekend Warrior may try is attempting to convince you that having alcohol out of your life is a bad thing. As time elapses and you start to feel happier and more in control of your life, you may see yourself missing the alcohol. It is not uncommon to start romanticizing the alcohol. So brace yourself for these moments. More than likely, you will experience some sadness over parting ways with your old "pal." It's almost like a bad break up. You know- you hate each other, and then you break up, but after some time apart you find yourself longing for that person and remembering all of the good times that you had together. Well, the same goes for alcohol. You may think you miss it sometimes, but just like your ex, that's only because you haven't been with it in awhile. You forgot about all of the pain and dysfunction he/she brought into your life, and how miserable you were with him/her, and how he/she slept with almost every single guy/girl in the... Wait a minute. Where was I going with this? Oh, yes; our Weekend Warriors have caused us a lot of pain and suffering and it is time to slay these beasts once and for all. We are now aware that alcohol is no longer a necessary part of our lives. In just a short time we have made a conscious decision to eliminate alcohol from our routines forever. If I may quote the venerable Taylor Alison Swift, "We are never ever, ever getting back together."

You have begun to take the initial steps to secure a happy and productive lifestyle for yourself. Now you will delve further into the depths of your inner being and find out who your Weekend Warrior is and who you really are. Learn your triggers and remain vigilant. You have surpassed the most difficult part of this transitional process. Sweet stuff, dudes and dudettes! Before you complete the questions and tasks that I have laid out for you in this chapter, take a look at this poem that I wrote many years ago about the internal struggle of alcohol consumption. I recite this to myself very often. It has sort of become a daily mantra of mine that helps me remain watchful of my mind's cravings so that I do not slip back into poor habits. Feel free to use this as a mantra of your own. And hey, while you are at it, why don't you go ahead and write one of your own. Now get to work. We are just getting started, you hydrated SOB. I'll see you in two weeks for Chapter III where we will discuss new habits, hobbies, and routines. Fly straight and have a great.

"An Internal War"

Be gone unholy savior

So never to succumb to your tempting pleasures again

May my mind stay vigilant and never waver

For this constant crave has proven arduous to amend

Sleepless nights have filled me with morning despair

Redundant settings no longer do I yearn for

For tell me how can a man truly fare

If he cannot win an internal war?

-Frank Hall

Getting to Know Your Weekend Warrior: Questions and Reflections

1. What are my triggers? List. Analyze. Reflect.

2. What non-alcoholic beverages do I enjoy while I am out now that I have retired from drinking?

3. How do I feel right now?

4. How do I like my new healthy and productive daily routines?

5. How have I managed to remain abstinent for my first two weeks?

- Remain Abstinent.
- Continue your healthy and productive daily routine. Document progress.

Challenges:

Plan an outdoor day adventure and fulfill it. It can be anything. Document your results.

Create a personal mantra. Recite Daily.

III

Habits, Hobbies, and Routines

ONE MONTH OF ABSTINENCE

"All great changes are preceded by chaos."

-Deepak Chopra

BY NOW YOU SHOULD BE SAILING smoothly. The storm is over and the winds are back in your sails. You are alcohol free and beginning to feel comfortable in your new healthy routines.

You may notice your feelings of sadness and regret have been replaced with motivation, determination, peace of mind, and most importantly happiness. You may be realizing that the problems that once seemed wildly out of control and unmanageable are now perfectly manageable. There are many reasons why you are starting to feel so great. Now that you are refraining from alcohol consumption, your body chemistry is realigning and essentially unfucking itself. I'm not much of scholar so if you want a more scientific answer to this conundrum other than "unfucking itself" feel free to Google it.

Now then, I can tell you in detail about a few other reasons why you may be feeling like Charlie Bucket upon entering the Chocolate Room in Roald Dahl's dreamy "Willy Wonka and the Chocolate Factory." Clarity my jubilant companions! Good ol' fashioned lucid and coherent clarity! You are now seeing the world with unhindered emotions again. Your behaviors should now be consistent with your true values and principles. Every decision that you are making is from a place of rationality and logic. Whether or not that is a good thing depends upon your rationality and logic. But the point is, you have found balance in your daily routines and you have more peace and stability in your life than you did when you were out gallivanting.

I want to touch on my earlier statement; "You may be realizing that the problems that once seemed wildly out of control and unmanageable are now perfectly manageable." Aside from seeing with clarity, I want you to think of another obvious reason for this. Time. You have more time. Just think of all the hours that you have been saving since the day you decided to stop poisoning yourself. Pretty awesome, right? Now you can start taking care of all of the things in your life that need to be taken care of and then some.

However, it is the "and then some" that we need to keep an eye on. Boredom is boring and having too much free time on our hands is no bueno. It is easier to fall back into our bad habits when we have too much spare time. And since we have promised ourselves that we will under no circumstances go back to those habits, we must find new hobbies to occupy that void. Well, what do you enjoy? Hiking, biking, weightlifting, team sports, yoga, meditation, reading, writing, painting, dancing, playing an instrument, volunteering, taking a class, etc. etc. etc. The list is endless. Go back to that inner child in you and find the things that naturally give you the excitement that you crave. Once you know what those things are, get yourself a new pair of Nike sneakers and just do it. (Really lame joke.) But seriously, just do it. Get up and go. Once you start immersing yourself in the activities that you truly enjoy, you will begin to meet other people who share those interests.

Ever get that sphere of influence speech from your parents after puking all over their bathroom after a night of drunken debauchery? Yeah? No? Well I did. And it really does make sense. Whether we are aware of it or not, we adopt a lot of the collective characteristics of the circles that we most closely surround ourselves with. This is not to say you must rid yourself of all of your friends, but it sure wouldn't hurt to start forming new relationships as well. We are carving out a new life for ourselves and we will want to surround ourselves with the people who are heading in the same direction that we are going. And who knows, some of your friends might even start following in your footsteps. Imagine that. You, a leader? Wouldn't that be something? Chances are you will be very helpful to many of your friends now that you are clear minded and level headed. But for the love of God, just remember to be cool. This is a friendly reminder to never become that damned condescending sober douche. Stay humble. Always stay humble. There is nothing worse than a CSD. You must understand that abstinence is something that we chose for ourselves. So before you board the "I'm better than you" train, just remember how annoying it is to listen to someone lecture you on how to live your life. Just because you chose a life of abstinence does not mean that everyone is going to want that for himself or herself. It is also important to note that you will more than likely have a greater impact on others by the way you conduct yourself and live your life in comparison to what you "preach." With that being said, lead by example and become your own hero before opening up your own church.

As far as new habits and hobbies are concerned, it does not take very long to form healthy and positive habits (approximately two to four weeks) but taking those initial steps is where the ultimate challenge lies. You need to be motivated. Sometimes extremely motivated. You need to forget about the snooze button on your cell phone and get moving. It is so hard to get started. I will not deny it. But once you are up and at 'em and the momentum shifts in your favor, your new habits and hobbies will naturally take shape. It just takes a little time for your mind and body to get used to these new changes. So keep at it. Repetition is the best way to reinforce any skill or behavior. You know, the old "practice makes perfect" proverb. That is why I challenged you to create a healthy and productive daily routine for yourself in chapter I. I cannot stress the importance of routines enough. I genuinely believe that a well-balanced morning routine is the foundation for a happy and successful lifestyle. The way that you start your morning off will influence the rest of your day in a major way. It has been said that if you win the morning you win the day. Allotting your time properly will reduce stress and keep you in sync with the world around you.

Synchronicity is a concept that was developed by well-known psychologist Carl Jung and is defined as being the simultaneous occurrence of events that appear significantly related but have no discernible causal connection. When you have a consistent routine, you will start to notice a certain rhythm to your day that you may not have been previously mindful of. I don't want to get overly hippie on you, but the feeling is comparable to floating through a sweet Mozart symphony. Whether it is getting all of the green lights on your morning drive to work or getting home just in time to catch a beautiful sunset, or even just a simple moment of bliss, you will become more aware that you are in sync with your world. Yes, these are only subtle examples and no, of course I am not saying that life will be perfect. But you can take solace in that with healthy, positive, and productive routines you will become more "in tune" and in touch with yourself and the world around you. Marcus Aurelius, a Roman Emperor and practitioner of the ancient philosophy known to us today as stoicism once said, "Constantly regard the universe as one living being, having one substance and one soul; and observe how all things have reference to one perception, the perception of this one living being; and how all things act with one movement; and how all things are the cooperating causes of all things which exist; observe too the continuous spinning of the thread and the contexture of the web." Synchronicity baby. Synchronicity.

You may have noticed that I keep throwing the word productive around when speaking of your daily routines and, yes, there is a reason for this. Think of your day today and answer this question: Were you occupying your time with activities for the sake of filling a void or were you actually being productive? As we start filling up our free time with fun activities for our leisure, it is also important that we incorporate some habits and hobbies into our day that make us productive as well. With keeping in mind the fact that, "All work and no play makes Jack a dull boy," we must find a healthy balance between work and leisure and between busyness and productivity.

As I stated earlier, your life is starting to become manageable now that you are one month free from alcohol. Roll with that positive momentum and use that to help carry you forward. Do not give into temptations now that your life is starting to get back on track. You do not want to slip back into the vicious cycle of abstinence followed by moderation followed by excessiveness. It is a slippery slope so keep that in mind. Refer back to the earlier chapters and to your own writings should you ever feel any desire or urge to drink. One month of sobriety is no joke, kiddo. You should really be proud of yourself and your accomplishments so far. Now let's keep building. Over the next month, answer the following questions and begin to find some new hobbies. Continue your daily routines. Keep reciting your mantras and positive affirmations. Focus on your goals. We will pick up in one month with Chapter IV in which we will talk about the benefits we have been experiencing and what else we can look forward to down the road. Fly straight and have a great.

Habits, Hobbies, and Routines: Questions and Reflections

1. What has been working for me lately?

2. How have I been filling up my free time?

3. What were some highlights of my first month of sobriety?

4. As a child, what were my favorite activities?

5. How have I handled myself in situations where alcohol was present?

- Do not drink alcohol.
- Continue documenting your daily routines.
- Stay busy and productive.
- Reread your reflections from previous chapters.

Challenge:

Find a new hobby that you think you will enjoy and give it your full attention. Document progress.

• IV •

Reaping The Benefits

TWO MONTHS OF ABSTINENCE

"The only way to make sense out of change is to plunge into it, move with it, and join the dance."

- Alan Watts

"YOU KNOW HOW MUCH I USED to love drinking right? Well I love everything about not drinking that much more." I remember saying this to a good friend of mine after a few months of abstinence and I truly meant it with every fiber of my being. When I first stopped my habitual drinking routines I really thought that this meant I was going to be bored and lonely a lot of the time. I was afraid that I would "miss out on all the fun" once alcohol was no longer in my life. Turns out life is a hell of a lot more fun without the booze. I finished up that statement to my friend with the humdrum yet meaningful expression, "Life is so amazing." I meant that. And it really is.

You are two months into slaying your Weekend Warrior and beginning to reap the fruits of your labor. The abundance of short-term benefits is stacking high. Your new routines and hobbies are helping you to become your true self, and now some of the long-term benefits are starting to show. Lets start with the one benefit that for whatever reason gets a lot of people the most excited. The money. The dough. The skrillah. The cheddar. The cabbage. The cold hard cash bay-bay! Ready for some arithmetic? I will lowball and say that on average you used to spend roughly $200 a week on alcohol and alcohol related purchases. By alcohol related purchases, I am referring to the junk food you ordered at 2 am, the annoying the hell out of your Uber driver rides, the late night impulse Amazon Prime drunk shopping, etc. At $200 a week you will be saving $800 a month, which brings us to $1600 in only two months. Yes my abstemious friends, that is a heaping $9,600 extra in your bank account after one year of abstinence. That's math. And here's the kicker—all you have to do is NOTHING. Retirement from alcohol has a pretty sweet pension package. Gnarly!

Ok, so now let's imagine that somebody told you they would give you $10k a year to quit drinking. I think most logical people would take a fellow up on that wager. So think of it like this: Right now you are in the position to make that hypothetical proposal a reality. All you have to do is continue to bet on yourself and save those chips for something worthwhile.

Although these next long term benefits may not be quite as important to you as the latter, I still want to briefly cover your overall physical health improvements and what not. (Get your priorities checked people.) You should now be experiencing superior sleeping patterns, a more functional immune system, clearer skin, and you might notice that you have a lot more energy. You have reduced your chances of getting heart and liver diseases, and you may be losing some serious weight if you didn't replace the drink with the cake. Just look back at a picture of yourself from two months ago and I am sure you will notice a significant difference in your appearance. You can literally feel the positive changes taking effect, and believe me it shows as well.

While you were partaking in alcohol consumption you were putting yourself at risk for numerous health problems. Unfortunately, our society's poor drinking habits are shoved so far under the rug that these alcohol related health issues could go unnoticed and untreated for months, years, or even decades. I think it is a crying shame that we are not doing more to educate the public about these seemingly normal drinking routines that are far from normal. These habits pose a much more serious threat than most people are aware of. But luckily for you, after two months of abstinence, most of the damage that you have done to your body from your alcohol consumption should now be repaired.

And how about your relationships with your family and friends? Oh yeah, that's a big one. Are they digging the changes that you have been making to your lifestyle? I am sure that you are making many of your loved ones so proud. As long as you aren't being the goddamned CSD, your relationships should be thriving more than they have ever before. This is because you are giving your very best self to them at all times. Now that's a great feeling.

Aside from saving a ton of cash, living healthy, feeling like a million bucks, looking sexy as ever, and being a coherent human being again, I have saved my personal favorite for last. You guessed it, the impact of abstinence on your mind. For starters, you are no longer drinking yourself stupid. I know, I know. That's a little bit harsh, but it's the stone cold truth. If you continued down the path that you were on, your brain functions would have progressively deteriorated over the span of your life. We all remember the short-term effects of alcohol on our brains from the nights that we were out getting as drunk as Cooter Brown. The slurred speech, the recklessness, the poor judgment, and the awful blackouts. It's a good thing we chose to nip this in the bud when we did, because the long-term effects of excessive alcohol consumption are down right dreadful. Cognitive thinking skills are greatly weakened and over time you could even experience moderate to severe brain damage. No buzz is worth the untimely loss of brainpower and the potential destruction of your mind.

Your mind is beautiful and unique. It is filled with creativity, ideas, loving emotions, and wonder. You have unlimited potential in your head, and after two months of sobriety you can really start to tap into its power. You have already seen what your mind is capable of. After all, it was your mind that enabled you to figure out how you would slay your Weekend Warrior in the first place. It was your mind that helped you triumph over your habitual drinking routines and replace them with healthy and productive ones. It is your mind that continues to guide your hand in each journal entry that you create throughout this course. Your perseverance and dedication have been exceptional. You have begun to reshape your life in accordance with your true self, and that is absolutely sensational.

Although I only mentioned a few benefits here, as you continue down your path of sobriety you will notice that there are countless rewards in remaining alcohol free. Conveniently enough, there might not even be a single negative effect from remaining abstinent. At least none that I am aware of. Looking back on it, the choice was always an obvious one. You just had to want it. You had to learn to embrace change, step out of your comfort zone and let your ego and pride get out of your own way. You believed in yourself and you must continue to believe in yourself. You deserve all of the blessings and happiness that have been coming, and will continue to come in your direction. In one month we will pick up with chapter V where we will discuss maintaining motivation for long-term abstinence. But until then, please answer the following questions and keep on shining. You have come so far in such a short time frame. Keep it up. Fly straight and have a great.

Reaping the Benefits: Questions and Reflections

1. What benefits of alcohol free living have you
    been experiencing?

2. What new hobbies have you taken on?

3. Have you made any adjustments to your daily routines?

4. Have you had any urges or desires to drink alcohol? If so,
    what strategies worked to resist these urges? If not, what do
    you think has served you best in suppressing any feelings
    of temptations?

5. What were some of your favorite memories from this
    past month?

    - No Alcohol.
    - Set some financial goals.
    - Continue to document your daily routines.
    - Be grateful each and every day.

Challenge:

Take the money that you would have spent in a week worth of alcohol and donate it to a charity of your choosing.

V

Maintaining Motivation

THREE MONTHS OF ABSTINENCE

"Growth is an erratic forward movement.
Two steps forward, one step back. Remember
that and be very gentle with yourself."

- Julia Cameron

MANY OF US HAVE HEARD OR uttered the words "high on life" to refer to the euphoric feelings that we get from the plenitude of natural pleasures that we experience after beginning a life of sobriety. These emotions of exaltation tend to become extreme when we initially adjust to our new and improved lifestyles. We have set high expectations for our future and have been exceptionally determined and motivated over the past few months. These feelings of motivation are imperative for maintaining a life of abstinence. But as time goes on and we become fully adjusted to our new lifestyles, some of the feelings of euphoria and determination might start to recede. There is actually a term for this known as "Pink Cloud Syndrome." Pink Cloud Syndrome refers to the happiness and overwhelming joy that is felt after starting a new life of sobriety. For a while things may appear to be all sunshine and rainbows, but as we continue down the road, the pink cloud may start to fade away. This could be very dangerous to our cause. Our Weekend Warriors have been kept at bay for quite sometime, but that does not mean that they are gone forever. Our Weekend Warriors are always lurking in the shadows. This is a warning that is not designed to frighten you. This is a warning that is designed to enlighten you. There is always work to be done.

If you start to notice or have already noticed that your pink cloud is dissolving, you must take action. Should this pertain to you, you must find out why you have been experiencing a lack of determination lately. Have you failed at accomplishing some of your goals? Are the problems in your life becoming too difficult to cope with on your own? Are you becoming bored with your new lifestyle? Ask yourself these questions, and get to the root of what is troubling you. You need to stay observant and remain in touch with your emotions at all times. Then you can get around the roadblocks and begin solving your problems with a sense of clarity.

Just know that you will get discouraged from time to time and there is nothing wrong with that. There will be days when you feel flustered and overwhelmed. At times, life will push you around and test you. It is easy to lose motivation and become lackadaisical if you do not remain watchful. Therefore, you must train yourself to be just as motivated and determined in the hard times as you are when everything is going your way. In the wise words of one of the most brilliant Roman philosophers, Seneca the Younger, "A setback has often cleared the way for greater prosperity. Many things have fallen only to rise to more exalted heights." With the right attitude, you will actually learn a great deal by persevering through the tough times. Some situations will seem impossible to overcome but you must fight that feeling. Turn that negative energy into positive fuel to propel you forward. On the other side of adversity there is prosperity. So when things don't go according to your plan, do not let it break you and take away from your progress. Use those moments as opportunities to strengthen yourself. Buck up and stay motivated.

Maybe you are still just as motivated as you were when we began at Ground Zero, and that is fantastic. Everyone's journey is different. Our stories may have similarities but each experience is unique. I want to take this moment to remind you that this book is just a guide, and it is you who is the master of your mind. You create your own destiny. You hold the key to your success. In this DIY workshop you have been the one behind the wheel. So continue to ask yourself the questions that you think will serve you best in remaining abstinent and motivated.

Whatever the case may be, it is time for you to reignite the fire under your ass. I want you to think back to the day that you decided to read this book. How did you feel? If you don't remember, go back and reread your journal entries. Read about your feelings of depression, anxiety, self-pity, sadness, shame, disgust, and heartbreak. I want you to dive deeply into the emotions that you felt in that moment when you finally said enough is enough. Think back to the day that you screamed, "I can't take this shit anymore!" and feel that pain. Pause for a moment to reflect. Now release it.

These are not your feelings today. You no longer have to feel that torment. You may not even be able to identify with the person that you were just three months ago. Each night before you go to bed, you should know that you have given your very best self to the world. You have plenty of time to work on achieving your goals. Do not get distracted from the amazing progress that you have made in a very short period of time.

Today I ask you to express gratitude for what you have in your life because of your decision to remain abstinent. Forget about your problems for a second. We all have problems. That's life. Take the time that you have set aside right now to fully appreciate your environment and be grateful that you are now healthy and living your life according to your true principles. Think of all that you have accomplished so far. Think of everyone and everything in your life that makes you happy. Give thanks for all of the wonderful blessings that you have right now. You deserve all of it.

This Pink Cloud bullshit is just that. Bullshit. We create it. We let it disappear. So don't let it disappear. This entire process has been far more than "quitting drinking." This process is about personal rediscovery. It is about finding ways to occupy your time in positive and productive ways. It is about harnessing the beautiful potential of your true self and unleashing it into the world. There is a multitude of ways for you to maintain motivation. Find the methods that strengthen you and master them. If you want to live in a pink cloud your whole life, go for it. If you want to sing Kelly Clarkson's hit single "Stronger" while you are in the shower, do it. Do whatever creams your twinkie. As long as the alcohol remains in the bottle and you aren't harming yourself or anybody else, do it. Continue to roll with the positive momentum in your life. Let go of any negative thoughts that come into your mind and keep them as distant as possible. You have made significant progress and you must know this.

Unfortunately, we cannot expect non-stop progress and success. There will be times in our lives where we must face necessary failure and defeat. But that does not mean that we need to let the failures of our lives define us or set us back anymore than they have to. We must continue to learn from our mistakes and find the strength and courage from within ourselves when we are experiencing these personal defeats. We have already proved that out of the darkest of days we can pull ourselves up from disparity and create the brightest of futures for ourselves. You must never allow your motivation to fade away. Continue onwards down the road of abstinence. It is a noble venture.

For one quarter of a year you have been free from the grips of habitual drinking routines. Alcohol is completely out of your life and your world is unquestionably clearer because of that.

In the past three months you have made exceptional progress, but it is critical to be reminded that you need to continue to advance yourself. It is never beneficial to become complacent in your lifestyle. With the proper balance of goal setting for your future and gratitude for your present situation, you will have a positive and peaceful experience as you continue to blossom. Now it is time to get out that journal and answer the corresponding questions for this chapter. In one month's time you will read the final chapter of this book and you will compile a list of your beliefs, principles, and passions. We will discuss your four-month personal journey as well as how to become your own hero once you have finished this course. Until then, fly straight and have a great.

Maintaining Motivation: Questions and Reflections

1. How will you remain motivated in hard times?

2. How do you feel in this moment?

3. What is the impact of your new habits and hobbies on your daily life?

4. What recent benefits have you been experiencing because of your alcohol free life?

5. Before and After: What is your life like now in comparison to what it was before you decided to live a life of abstinence?

Challenge:

If you haven't already, take a look at some of the quotations in this book. Most of the people that I have cited are authors, philosophers, and poets. Find the one quotation that speaks to you most directly and do some research on that author. Find something that interests you and purchase one of their works.

VI

Becoming Your Own Hero

FOUR MONTHS OF ABSTINENCE
AND BEYOND

"The only journey is the journey within."

-Rainer Maria Rilke

WHAT ARE SOME OF THE EXCEPTIONAL qualities of your heroes and role models? Think of all of the positive attributes that make you gravitate towards them. Whether they are fictional characters, real life trailblazers, or personal heroes in your own life, I want you to discover exactly what it is about them that inspires you and helps fuel your soul. I want you to tap into the powerful emotions that you feel when you are learning through these individuals. Do they provide you with hope? Do they make you feel courageous? Do they give you a sense that anything in this world is possible? Yeah? Well that's good news because everything is possible. Ever since the day that you vowed to remain abstinent and slay your Weekend Warrior you too have been inspiring people, maybe even without realizing it. After months of extensive self-reflection you have built an arsenal of wisdom, discipline, and strength. You have rediscovered your true passions. You are now on a beautiful new path that you are continuously paving for yourself each and every day. You have successfully slain your Weekend Warrior but the journey has just begun. Your personal growth process should never come to an end. William Blake, an English poet during the Romantic Age once said, "Ability may take you to the top, but it takes character to stay there." Your persistence has helped guide you in accomplishing your goal of an alcohol free life and now it will be your consistence that will enable you to maintain that stability. Persistence plus consistence is a recipe for success in anything that you decide to set your mind to.

You must continue broadening your own horizons as well as serving as a guiding light in the lives of your fellow brothers and sisters. You will also be extremely beneficial to those who seek your guidance and may be struggling with their own personal issues. Through your own personal growth process you have developed the ability to share your story as well as the capability of providing others with a sense of direction. You have everything you need right inside of you to be a modern day hero on a daily basis. Now I'm not talking about fighting crime in the mean streets of Gotham City, or risking your limbs by trying to convince Darth Vader that there is still good in him. I'm talking about some real life, gritty, down to Earth Mother Teresa shit. Don't be mistaken; I am not expecting you all to be saints here. However, I am expecting you all to be leaders in your own right. It is my wish for you to lead a selfless life filled with acts of kindness and thoughtfulness. You are ready to become your own hero. And in becoming your own hero you will become a role model and a hero to many others along the way. As long as you conduct yourself in a manner that is in permanent accordance with your true self, you will not have much trouble finding peace in the chaotic world around you. Lead by example and remain humble. Never become the CSD. Be selfless, stay motivated, give love, and most importantly be happy. It is now time for me to leave you with your final task in this workshop: Your Code of Honor.

You will develop a personal Code of Honor that should embody the life that you wish to live, the impression that you want to make on strangers and your loved ones alike, and the legacy that you wish to leave behind. By creating a Code of Honor, you will be able to further improve the qualities of yourself that you need to work on. You will also be able to expand upon your beautiful characteristics and strengths. This will be a list and assessment of your beliefs, values, morals, principles, and anything that you believe is pivotal in creating a life of abundant peace, happiness, and success. I will share with you my Code of Honor in the hope that it can serve as a template that will enlighten you to follow many of these uplifting and fruitful principles. This is just a guide. As I have often made clear, we are all individuals and every situation is wonderfully unique. Every person is different. Our belief systems and philosophies may overlap in some instances and be conflicting in others. And that is totally fine. After all, it is just different flavors of ice cream. Everybody wants to be happy, but there is no perfect equation. We must all "find our own way" so to speak.

It is only through your own personal discoveries that your Code of Honor will naturally manifest itself with your feelings. Over time, you will be able to refer back to your code in any situation where you must confront life decisions and conflicts. Your code should be constantly evolving and growing with you throughout your life. Always strive to be your very best self and seek the truth from within.

Well, it has been one hell of a ride hasn't it? You saw this through to the very end and hopefully you see the enormity in this personal achievement. Four months free from the heavy chains that once held you down. Four months independent from the deceptive poison that continuously held you back from reaching your full potential. Four months liberated from a useless and unnecessary substance that will never bring any true happiness or prosperity into your life. Four months of learning, growing, and commitment. Four months of truth seeking, newfound passions, clarity, courage, wisdom, and honor. Four months of low valleys and high peaks. Four months of personal reflection, dedication, perseverance, and success. You did it. But you must continue to do it. Every day new obstacles will present themselves and you must continue to prepare for them. Love yourself, love your brothers and sisters, love the world you live in, and become your own hero! For the final time, fly straight and have a great.

My Code of Honor

Daily Mantra:

Love.

Peace.

Clarity.

Wisdom.

Strength.

Give Love. Love your family and friends and make sure they know that they are loved by you. It is so important to allow love to pour out of you and into the world every chance you get. You have a big heart and you can spread so much happiness just by giving all of your love.

Spread peace, hope, and positivity. I once read somewhere that peace does not mean to be in a place where there is no noise, trouble or hard work. It means to be in the midst of those things and still be calm in your heart. True peace comes from within you. This is the truth. You cannot attain peace from anywhere else but inside of yourself. As far as hope and positivity are concerned, you need to be a light that shines throughout the day. Be cheerful and optimistic. Your thoughts are powerful and with a positive mindset, you will attract a lot more of the things that you want in your life.

Stay grateful and thankful. Appreciate everything you have in your life. No matter what your situation is, there are people and things in your life that you must never take for granted. Life owes you nothing and guarantees you nothing but death. If you want to continue to accomplish your goals you must be happy with the things you already have or you may find yourself constantly craving more. Don't get trapped in the "I'll be happy when..." box. Be happy and thankful for what you have now and always.

Create and maintain healthy, positive, and productive routines. Routines can keep the human machine running smoothly. Once you adapt to a routine it will become automatic. So make your routines as healthy as possible to ensure that you don't form bad habits along the way.

Don't react to situations. When something happens that is out of your control, do not be quick to react. A lot of the time that is a fool's mistake. Allow yourself a moment to consider your approach and then act. Make sure your intentions for your actions are good hearted, especially when dealing with other people. We are here to strengthen each other not to belittle each other.

Make life easier for others. This can be done in many ways. Overall, just be conscious of your surroundings and try to help people out to the best of your ability. Be kind and light hearted. Life is too short to be any other way.

Endure. Endurance is one of your best strengths. This is what separates you from the herd. You may not be the biggest or strongest person out there, but your ability to suffer patiently is beyond the limits of many people. Use the struggles you face to empower yourself and others.

Meditate. Daily meditation is key. A morning transcendental meditation and an evening mindfulness meditation are extremely rewarding. The TM will help you keep your focus on your affirmations in the morning, which will keep your mind present and focused throughout your day. The MM will help you to relax and return to the still self at night. This has been a beautiful balance in my life.

Hike. Hiking is by far my favorite hobby. I could legitimately do some form of hiking/backpacking every day. Returning to nature gives me so much satisfaction that it is indescribable in many cases. There is true freedom in the wilderness and it has without a doubt helped strengthen my mind, body, and soul.

Take baths. I am a firm believer that everyone should take a twenty-minute bath every damn day. Most of my early morning transcendental meditations are done in a hot bath and it is one of the most peaceful ways to start or end the day. I am so serious when I say that I believe if more people took baths the world would be a significantly better place.

Eat healthy. Forget diets. Just consistently eat healthy. Leave room for dessert and cheat meals but stay away from the garbage. You can't go wrong with eggs and oatmeal for breakfast and grilled chicken and brown rice for lunch and dinner.

Exercise. I'll do the weightlifting from time to time, but for me it's yoga all the way. I have worked manual labor jobs for over a decade and yoga has made my body feel incredible. I am also very much into the mental aspect of yoga. I enjoy the healing and singing bowls, the breathing techniques, as well as the ancient philosophies and traditions that go hand in hand with the physical practice.

Accept criticism. Ignore judgment. Don't be afraid to listen to criticism. You can learn a lot from someone else's perspective on situations. Advice doesn't always need to be taken but it should always be respected and internalized. Use your discernment and common sense to determine what advice will benefit you and what will not. As far as judgment, don't feed into it. There will always be judgmental people out there and most of the time their predetermined minds are already made up and nothing that you do or say will convince them otherwise. You don't want to work yourself up by talking to a person that is more interested in proving their point rather than being willing to learn from one another.

Be present-minded. Live in the moment. Do not fear the future. Do not dwell in the past.

Accept death. At the end of the road, nothing is permanent so love while you can! Enjoy every moment with the people and places that you associate yourself with. In most cases you will not have the opportunity to properly say goodbye when that time comes. Tomorrow is never promised. Also, do not be afraid of death. It's coming for us all so embrace that fact.

Write. Write whatever you feel compelled to. Continue to journal and write poetry. The more you do it, the better you will get. Writing gets your creative thoughts out into the physical world and helps your brain functions. Writing is very therapeutic for you.

Be forgiving. People fuck up all the time. So do you. Don't hold anything against people. If they did something to hurt you or your loved ones, explain your feelings in an articulate manner. Don't make them feel bad for their actions. Just let them know how it made you feel and forgive every chance you can.

Listen. Don't engage in conversation for the sake of hearing yourself talk. Listen and learn from others as often as you can.

Learn new skills. Try to attempt new things and tackle new projects when you have free time. The more skills you acquire throughout your life, the easier your life will be and the more fun you will have as well.

Be flexible to different and new ways of performing tasks. There is always more than one route towards achieving an objective. Don't get stuck in your own ways. Especially when you are working with somebody, it is important to work together and not against each other. Try to find the most efficient way to accomplish what you set out to do.

Adapt. You are very adaptable. You can thrive in many different environments with people of all walks of life. That is a major strength to have. It is beneficial to be easy going and find peace and comfort in all situations.

Embrace change. Don't be afraid of leaving your comfort zone. It is so important for personal growth.

Be early. Arrive at least fifteen minutes early to everything you do. Aside from being ahead of schedule, fifteen minutes is the perfect amount of time to adjust to your environment and prepare yourself for what lies ahead.

Expect nothing. Don't expect things to always go your way. Don't expect people to act the way that you think they will. The less expectations you have the better. It is ok to plan ahead or to make certain deductions, but don't always try to predict the exact outcome of an uncertain future. This will protect you from being let down when things don't go accordingly.

Eliminate emotions of fear, anger, and doubt. These emotions are absolutely useless in every single instance. Train your mind to eliminate them from your life. They serve no purpose.

Think, speak, and act with clarity and a unifying purpose. Everything you do should be clear. From your initial thoughts and feelings to the actions that respond with them. Find a purpose in your life and let everything you do coincide with that purpose.

Don't live in excess. Live comfortably within your means and find balance in all aspects of your life.

Embrace the differences in people. Everyone is unique and that is one of the most beautiful things about the world. It is our differences that help us grow together. Be loving and respectful to everyone.

Learn to fall in love with the things that you don't like if they are required of you. If you have to do something and there is no way to avoid doing it, you might as well learn to love it or you will go through the rest of your life dreading something that you have to do anyway.

Be disciplined. Tame your desires and be patient. Allow yourself to act at the appropriate moments. Be an embodiment of character and conviction. Follow your Code and stay vigilant.